Remember When...

The Funniest Book with the Word 'MILLENNIUM' on the Cover

The Comedy Team Mack & Jamie

Illustrations by Mack Dryden

LONGSTREET
Atlanta, Georgia

Published by
LONGSTREET PRESS, INC.
A subsidiary of Cox Newspapers
A subsidiary of Cox Enterprises, Inc.
2140 Newmarket Parkway
Suite 122
Marietta, GA 30067
www.lspress.com

Printed in the United States of America

1st printing 1999

Library of Congress Catalog Card Number: 99-61759

ISBN: 1-56352-584-4

Illustrations: Mack Dryden
Book design: Megan Wilson

DEDICATION

Thanks to the love and laughter of my entire family who
for some reason still think I'm funny.

—Jamie

I'd like to thank: My wife Teri for inspiring me, and for pretending not to
be too sleepy to listen to one more *Remember When* joke; my mom Neva,
who not only let me draw in church when I was a kid, but encouraged it;
my dad Herb who, in addition to giving me my sense of humor, paid for
my education and never complained once that it didn't lead to a real job;
and my manager Barry, who prevents me from completely destroying my
career about once a day.

—Mack

INTRODUCTION

Remember all those '70s weirdos carrying signs proclaiming "The end is near"? Well, turns out they were right. Along with rotary phones and the spotted owl, drugstore soda fountains and virgin brides, the only millennium we've ever known is about to end. It'll be history on January 1, 2001.

Appropriately for current American culture (which some consider an oxymoron), on January 1, 2000 most of us will celebrate the fake millennium, or the "Milli Vanilleum."

The Second Millennium will take down with it our beloved Twentieth Century, that span of years when tattooed cigar smokers went from being old and smelly to young and trendy; when personal trainers switched from horses to people; and when a tanning salon ceased to be hung with beaver pelts.

So it is only proper that before we slide blindly into the unknown Third Millennium, we should take a moment to recall some of the things we're leaving behind. Come with us as we... *Remember When!*

To Michael & Maryann,

Remember When...

...our lives were empty because we didn't know you?
Enjoy,

Mark

—a SMART BOMB was the one that chased
Wile E. Coyote around corners?

●●●

—DIGITAL COMMUNICATION was what you
used when somebody cut you off in traffic?

●●●

—if you got BEEPED, you were daydreaming
at a green light?

Remember When...

—GANGSTA RAP was what they rolled
Jimmy Hoffa up in?

Remember When...

—a MATTRESS CLEARANCE occurred when your girlfriend's husband came home unexpectedly?

●●●

—PAINTBALL was the annual dance for Sherwin-Williams employees?

Remember When...

—a WONDERBRA was one that a seventeen-year-old boy could remove in the dark with one hand?

●●●

—a SATELLITE DISH was dinnerware with a space motif?

Remember When...

—"SOCCER MOM" was what you yelled when a fight broke out at a Little League game?

Remember When...

—MOUSSE IN YOUR HAIR meant you were in serious trouble in the north woods?

Remember When...

—the only HOLISTIC FOOD we knew about
was Swiss cheese?

●●●

—you thought an OXYMORON was
an eight-sided idiot?

Remember When...

—a HARD DRIVE was 100 miles to grandma's with three kids pumped up on Easter candy?

●●●

—a HIP REPLACEMENT was a really cool substitute teacher?

Remember When...

—you thought a DOUBLE GRANDE FRAPPACCINO was a figure skater's big finish?

Remember When...

—a SOUND CARD was the one you pinned to your bicycle spokes for that motorcycle effect?

●●●

—WINDOWS 98 was a pigeon's scorecard?

Remember When...

—a FOOD PROCESSOR had a
hair net and a mole?

Remember When...

—SAFE SEX meant all the car doors were locked?

●●●

—you CELEBRATED DIVERSITY by trying
all 31 flavors?

●●●

—teenagers wore underwear UNDER
what they wore?

Remember When...

—a CARJACKER was a tool you
kept in the trunk?

●●●

—the only way to get a CELL PHONE
was to bribe the warden?

●●●

—BALLING ALL NIGHT meant
crying your eyes out?

Remember When...

—the THIGHMASTER was the
high school make-out king?

Remember When...

—FACTORY AIR came out of a smokestack?

●●●

—GETTING STONED left you dead
or badly bruised?

Remember When...

—PHONE SEX was when you tied her
up with the cord?

●●●

—SECONDHAND SMOKE was what came
out of a burning thrift store?

●●●

—AROMATHERAPY was Vicks VapoRub?

Remember When...

—a CHAT ROOM was the local beauty shop?

●●●

—GOVERNMENT WHISTLE-BLOWER was the leader of the Marine Corps Marching Band?

●●●

—a CARPOOL was a raffle for a Buick?

Remember When...

—TIGER WOODS was where you told your little brother you'd leave him if he didn't stop following you?

●●●

—a FREQUENT FLIER PROGRAM was "Sky King"?

—TRACK LIGHTING is what kept the horses
from running into each other?

Remember When...

—a SNOWBOARD was what you wedged under your tire to get going again?

Remember When...

—SPICE GIRLS sold curry in Bombay?

●●●

—a REGISTERED SEX OFFENDER was a nymphomaniac who wanted you to know where you could buy her a piece of wedding china?

Remember When...

—a REDI-TELLER was your big-mouthed,
back-fence neighbor?

●●●

—having enough RAM meant you were
sick of eating mutton?

●●●

—the PSYCHIC NETWORK was how all our
Moms knew what we were up to?

Remember When...

—PLASTIC SURGERY was fixing a broken yard flamingo?

●●●

—a STATIONARY BIKE was the one in the garage with two flat tires?

●●●

—OVERNIGHT DELIVERY meant she had a short labor?

Remember When...

—you had to buy a ticket to see
a PURPLE-HAIRED WOMAN with tattoos
and a pierced tongue?

Remember When...

—a MOTHERBOARD was the one she spanked you with?

•••

—RECYCLING was when you forgot something and had to ride your bike back to the store?

Remember When...

—MODEM was what you did to shaggy lawns?

●●●

—CALLER I.D. was established by looking
through the front-door peephole?

—REMOTE described a place where you could get lost, and not the darn thing that's *always* lost?

Remember When...

—SILICON VALLEY was a starlet's cleavage?

Remember When...

—the INFORMATION AGE was the year a teenager decided he/she knew everything?

●●●

—a SEARCH ENGINE was a Comanche scout?

Remember When...

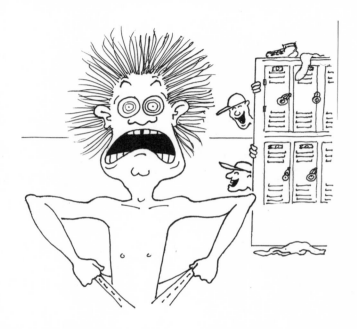

—a SHOCK JOCK was an athletic supporter
that had been dipped in ice water?

Remember When...

—a LAPTOP COMPUTER was a trashy secretary who was good with numbers?

●●●

—CHANNEL SURFING was how English beachboys got to France?

Remember When...

—PRESCHOOL meant *home*?

●●●

—trying to DOWNLOAD YOUR FLOPPY meant you were looking for a men's room?

●●●

—you had an INNER CHILD only if you were pregnant?

Remember When...

—CHAOS THEORY was the idea that having three toddlers couldn't be any worse than having two?

●●●

—TREADMILLS were used only by hamsters?

●●●

—SPAGHETTI STRAPS kept the pasta organized?

Remember When...

—ROLLERBLADES were those things used to cut pizza?

●●●

—an OUTING was a *family* thing?

Remember When...

—the only people who wore ridiculously BAGGY PANTS worked for Ringling Brothers?

Remember When...

—the PRESIDENT'S CUP was worn once a year,
during softball season?

Remember When...

—an attempt at HAIR RESTORATION was chasing your toupee in a windstorm?

●●●

—a GRUNGE BAND was ring-around-the-collar?

Remember When...

—a HOMELESS PERSON was a guitar player who'd just broken up with his girlfriend?

●●●

—BLACKENED SEA BASS washed up onshore after an oil spill?

●●●

—there were more MICROBREWERIES in the Kentucky hills than in San Francisco?

Remember When...

—CARPOOL TUNNEL SYNDROME was when you went crazy commuting to Manhattan with five co-workers?

●●●

—people lived off the land, and FAST FOOD was a panicked rabbit?

●●●

—EXTREME GAMES were played on Lambeau Field with a wind chill of -30°?

Remember When...

—N.O.W. meant when she'd better bring the B.E.E.R.?

40

Remember When...

—the only place you found BOTTLED WATER was in a fallout shelter?

●●●

—people got TATTOOS to set themselves *apart* from the crowd?

Remember When...

—INSTANT REPLAY was a Sanka burp?

●●●

—the fans did DRUGS and SILLY DANCES,
and not the players?

Remember When...

—CRUISE CONTROL was what obsessed the social director on the Queen Mary?

43

Remember When...

—GOING POSTAL meant you were in no hurry
for the package to get there?

●●●

—a LOW-IMPACT WORKOUT was just *watching* a
Jane Fonda tape?

Remember When...

—a WEB BROWSER was someone
shopping for a duck?

Remember When...

—a NINETEEN-INCH MONITOR was the shortest kid in the hall?

Remember When...

—MANDATORY SENTENCES were the ones you had to write for throwing spitballs in class?

●●●

—SELF STORAGE was a mausoleum?

Remember When...

—you went OUTSIDE for fresh air and INSIDE to smoke?

●●●

—a PROFESSIONAL ATHLETE CHARGED WITH A CRIME was news?

Remember When...

—a SPORTS BRA was one that even a
linebacker could unhook?

49

Remember When...

—SURFING THE NET was an evasive tactic used by a mackerel?

●●●

—somebody whose nose and eyebrows were PIERCED WITH METAL had just been in a car crash?

Remember When...

—GLOBAL WARMING was achieved when
Dolly Parton put on a wool sweater?

—anybody who belonged to a HEALTH CLUB was a nudist?

●●●

—there was only COFFEE-flavored coffee?

●●●

—a RING IN YOUR BELLY BUTTON meant you missed a place with your washcloth?

Remember When...

—MICROSOFT was a condition that kept men from enjoying mixed skinny-dipping?

●●●

—SEXUAL EQUALITY was when you finished at the same time?

●●●

—a VIRTUAL PET was an "Amazing Sea-Monkey"?

—MEN WERE FROM MARS and they by-God *liked* it there?

●●●

—INTERNET was whur she'd put her hair 'fore she went to work at the diner?

Remember When...

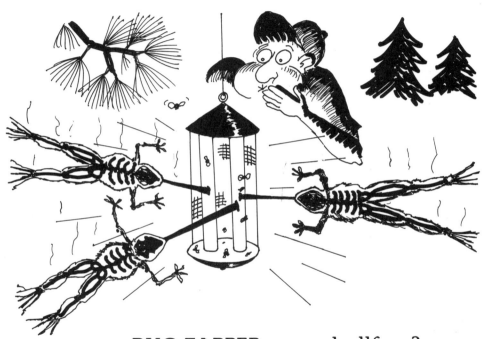

—a BUG ZAPPER was a bullfrog?

—LIPOSUCTION
was how a kid got a
Coke bottle stuck on
his tongue?

Remember When...

—getting ready to SMOKE A GOOD CUBAN meant you were going to try to kill Ricky Ricardo?

● ● ●

—PAY-PER-VIEW cost a quarter and you had to look through a peephole?

Remember When...

—a CLASS ACTION SUIT was that classy number you wore to get some action?

Remember When...

—the only FERTILITY DRUG you could give her
was a double martini?

●●●

—HIP HOP was what you did when you *really*
had to pee?

Remember When...

—a GAG ORDER was a doctor's command to induce vomiting?

●●●

—the only drugs for IMPOTENCE were the ones that made you laugh so much you couldn't have sex anyway?

Remember When...

—COSMETIC SURGERY was the only way
Tammy Faye Bakker could get hers off?

Remember When...

—using ARTIFICIAL INTELLIGENCE was how you bluffed your way through the essay question?

●●●

—your REAR-WINDOW DEFOGGER was Grandma's hankie?

●●●

—a LUXURY SPORTS VEHICLE was a Jeep with a heater?

Remember When...

—DEEP-TISSUE MASSAGE was a clumsy attempt to get that last Kleenex from the bottom of the box?

●●●

—a BUSINESS MODEL appeared on a car parts calendar in a bikini?

●●●

—a CODEPENDENT was a bogus name you added to get a bigger tax deduction?

Remember When...

—a NO-FLY ZONE was the area around your uncle's rocking chair that he could reach with his swatter?

●●●

—your LIQUID ASSETS consisted of two six-packs and a quart of tequila?

Remember When...

—a BAR CODE was a list of the rules of the tavern?

Remember When...

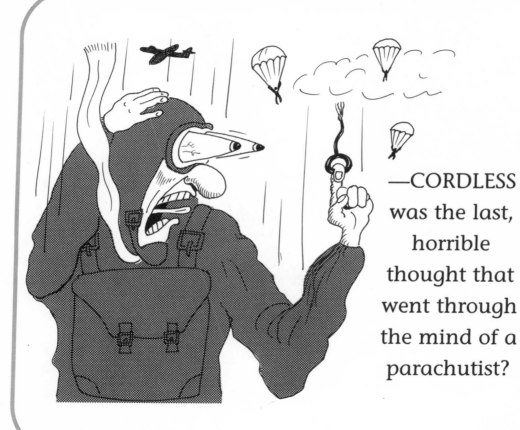

—CORDLESS was the last, horrible thought that went through the mind of a parachutist?

Remember When...

—KEYLESS ENTRY meant a burglary in progress?

●●●

—a TANNING SALON was hung with beaver pelts?

Remember When...

—MEGAHERTZ is what you got when you stubbed your little toe on a cast-iron bedstead?

Remember When...

—a DESK JET was a scale model of a Boeing 747?

●●●

—the STANDARD PRENUPTIAL AGREEMENT was that you'd wait 'til the honeymoon?

Remember When...

—a LONG DISTANCE CARRIER was a
cross-country trucker with hepatitis?

●●●

—a SUPPORT GROUP was the bottom line
in a cheerleader pyramid?

Remember When...

—POWER WINDOWS were paint-stuck and sprained your back?

Remember When...

—a NICOTINE PATCH was a plot out back where you grew a little for personal use?

●●●

—a DESIGNATED DRIVER was a three-iron?

●●●

—GENETIC ENGINEERING was going to M.I.T. because your father did?

Remember When...

—a MAXI-PAD was a *huge* apartment in the city?

●●●

—TIMESHARE was when you and a buddy pooled your money to buy a Bulova?

●●●

—an ORGAN TRANSPLANT meant another church had bought it?

Remember When...

—REBATE was when you put on a new worm?

•••

—a REPRODUCTION CENTER was the mimeograph room?

Remember When...

—a MAGNETIC STRIP was a mesmerizing dance?

Remember When...

—your HOME SECURITY SYSTEM shed on the couch and chewed your shoes?

Remember When...

—the RIPPLE EFFECT was achieved with a three-dollar bottle of wine?

●●●

—SUBSTANCE ABUSE was when you mixed your vegetables into a disgusting mess so your parents wouldn't make you eat them?

—GAY DIVORCÉE wasn't a contradiction in terms?

●●●

—the CABLE GUY was a Flying Wallenda?

Remember When...

—FANNY PACK was how obese people got into airline seats?

Remember When...

—you expected to see WINGS on your parakeet
but not on your sanitary pad?

●●●

—SWIPING A CREDIT CARD was a felony?

Remember When...

—a SCREEN SAVER kept the cat from shredding the back door?

Remember When...

—NETWORKING was trying to find something worth watching on the only three channels you had?

●●●

—a PERSONAL ORGANIZER was your mom?

Remember When...

—a SPIN DOCTOR came in to help
Scott Hamilton with his rotations?

Remember When...

—PRIVATE SCREENING was rubbing SPF 30 on your tender parts?

●●●

—IN-LINE SKATING was a conga line at the rink?

●●●

—LASER HAIR REMOVAL meant a close call for Luke Skywalker?

Remember When...

—E-MAIL was the loser she went out with after discarding males 'A' through 'D'?

●●●

—WINDOWS FOR DUMMIES had opening instructions printed right on the glass?

●●●

—an AIR PURIFIER was a box of matches on the back of the toilet?

—a FACE PEEL was an illegal
move in pro wrestling?

Remember When...

—anybody who built a HOT TUB was a
moonshiner?

●●●

—a PASSENGER-SIDE AIRBAG was your
brother-in-law?

Remember When...

—ROAMING CHARGES were filed when a parolee strayed too far?

●●●

—a RAP ARTIST worked in a department store during the Christmas holidays?

Remember When...

—JOGGING was something you did only to your memory?

Mack Dryden and Jamie Alcroft have been a comedy team since 1979. They hosted their own syndicated show, *Comedy Break*, and have made dozens of appearances on such shows as the *Tonight Show*, *Caroline's Comedy Club*, and *An Evening at the Improv*. Over the years, they have starred in television movies, appeared in commercials, radio skits, and voice-overs, and hosted numerous corporate awards ceremonies. Their recent play *Two for All* garnered rave reviews from the *Los Angeles Times*. They are currently working on a screenplay.

For more information on Mack and Jamie visit their website at:
www.mackandjamie.com